This Book Belongs To:

Bienvenue!

Welcome to our Paris adventure!

In this coloring book, you'll meet adorable girls exploring the magical city of Paris, France.

Paris is known as the "City of Light" because it was one of the first cities to have street lights.

You can visit the Eiffel Tower, a giant iron tower that sparkles at night, or see the Mona Lisa at the Louvre Museum, which is the biggest art museum in the world.

Get ready to color and discover the wonders of Paris!

Eiffel Tower

When you think of Paris, France
you probably have visions of the Eiffel Tower in your head!

It is super tall, standing at 1,083 feet high,
which is as tall as 108 grown-up giraffes standing on top of each other!
You can climb up its 1,665 steps, but there's also an elevator if you get tired.

At night, the Eiffel Tower sparkles and twinkles with
lots of bright lights, like a beautiful nightlight for the city.

Named after Gustave Eiffel, the super smart builder and engineer who
designed it, the tower welcomes millions of visitors every year,
making it one of the most famous places in the whole world.

Did You Know?!
The top of the Eiffel Tower is used to study weather.

The Eiffel Tower is like the crown jewel of Paris,

Haussmann Architechture

Haussmann architecture in Paris is super cool! A long time ago, a man named Baron Haussmann helped make Paris look fancy and beautiful. He designed big, wide streets and grand buildings with pretty balconies and lots of windows. The buildings have neat stone walls and are usually the same height, making them look like they're holding hands all through the city. Haussmann also added lots of parks and gardens, so there's always a lovely green place to play or relax. Thanks to Haussmann, Paris looks like a city from a fairy tale, with its beautiful, elegant buildings everywhere you go!

The rooftops of these Haussmann buildings are just as beautiful as the buildings themselves!

The zinc rooftops and chimney pots in Paris are really special! The rooftops are made of shiny, silvery zinc, and they make the city look like it's sparkling, especially when the sun shines on them. The rooftops have funny little chimney pots sticking out of them. These chimney pots are like tiny hats for the buildings, and they help smoke from fireplaces go outside. People who take care of the rooftops are called "zinc workers," and they're like acrobats, climbing high up on the buildings to keep everything looking nice and neat. They make sure the rooftops stay shiny and the chimney pots stay in good shape, so Paris always looks beautiful from above!

SS

Getting Around Paris

Getting around Paris is both fun and convenient.

The Metro trains are like a web of underground tracks
that can quickly take you to different parts of the city.
You can easily get on and off at various stops to visit famous places.
And, some of the underground Metro stations are so big,
you'll find things like markets and newspaper stands.

There are also buses that travel through the streets,
making it easy to reach your destination while enjoying the view.

Walking is another great option because
Paris has so many beautiful streets, parks, and cafes to discover.

Whether you choose to ride the Metro, take a bus,
or explore on foot, Paris is an exciting city to navigate!

Made in the USA
Columbia, SC
06 December 2024